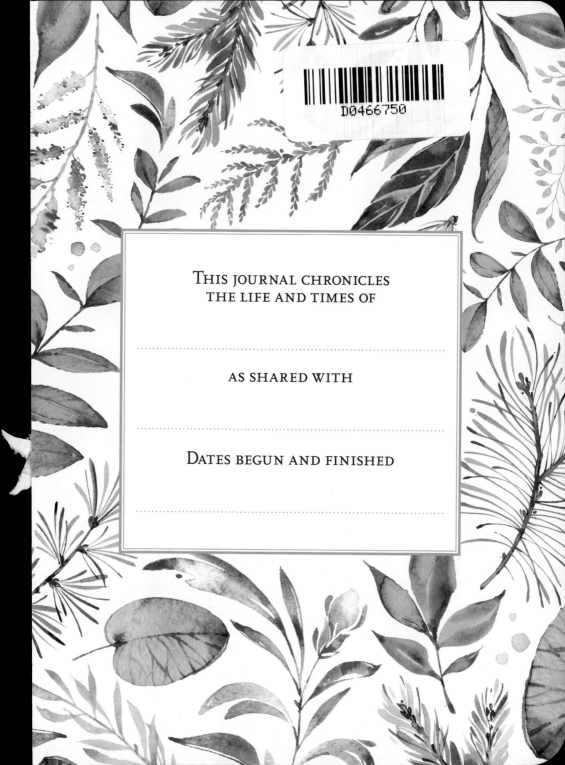

THIS JOURNAL CHRONICLES
THE LIFE AND TIMES OF

....

AS SHARED WITH

....

DATES BEGUN AND FINISHED

....

An Oral
HISTORY
Preserve Your Family's Story

Paula Spencer Scott

PETER PAUPER PRESS, INC.
WHITE PLAINS, NEW YORK

PETER PAUPER PRESS
Fine Books and Gifts Since 1928

OUR COMPANY

In 1928, at the age of twenty-two, Peter Beilenson began printing books on a small press in the basement of his parents' home in Larchmont, New York. Peter—and later, his wife, Edna—sought to create fine books that sold at "prices even a pauper could afford."

Today, still family owned and operated, Peter Pauper Press continues to honor our founders' legacy—and our customers' expectations—of beauty, quality, and value.

For Jim, improver of life stories

Designed by Heather Zschock
Image on pages 12-13 used under license from Shutterstock.com

Copyright © 2018
Peter Pauper Press, Inc.
202 Mamaroneck Avenue
White Plains, NY 10601 USA
All rights reserved
ISBN 978-1-4413-2781-9
Printed in China
7 6 5

Visit us at www.peterpauper.com

Table of Contents

Memory...

IS THE DIARY THAT WE ALL
CARRY ABOUT WITH US.

—*Oscar Wilde*

INTRODUCTION

A Memorable Gift

*Nobody ever regretted having captured the
details of a family story on paper.*

Memories grow fuzzy. Relationships slip away. Stories go untold. Even important facts like wedding dates, a childhood home address, or the "secret" ingredient to Grandma's chili can fade away in less than a generation. If you've ever puzzled over the nameless, unrecognizable faces in an old photo, you know this frustrating feeling of loss.

And a pixelated face alone won't give you the fuller, 3-D portrait of the person: their likes and dislikes, wishes and regrets, quirks and contributions, everyday habits and major life milestones. What was their outlook on life? What wisdom did they collect over the years? What, and who, influenced them and mattered most?

These are the bits and pieces parents and adult children don't always get around to talking about in the busy course of daily life. Even things we "know," we risk forgetting. Other details we never knew, and eventually lose the chance to retrieve.

To preserve that rounder, richer sense of a person you love, you have to ask.

To keep it alive and shareable with future generations, you have to write it down.

Being intentional about recording an oral history is a gift. It's a gift to the person in focus. It's a gift to you. As you open a window into your parent's or grandparent's life, you might glean useful insights into your own family life. Not least, having a life captured on paper is both a gift to the ancestors in your family tree and, especially, a gift to descendants—the grandchildren and others not even born yet.

How to Use This Book

This journal is designed for an adult child to record the story of a parent or grandparent. (You can also use it to record someone else's oral history.)

In its pages, you'll find a mix of fill-in-the-blanks, quick prompts, and open-ended questions. Some are meant to record factual information. Others encourage reminiscences, opinions, and the chance to share hard-won advice. **Please note:** The "you" in these questions and prompts refers to the parent, or other subject, of this oral history.

Interspersed throughout are some repeating sections. These invite the subject to share **Favorites** (a quick list), offer **Words of Advice** (everyone really wants to know!), answer a speedy **Yes or No**, and reminisce about culture and recent history in segments that ask, "**Do you remember...?**" There's also blank space to save "**Standout Memories**" of various times and places.

All the prompts are loosely organized into eight themed chapters, from ancestry and early life to milestones, celebrations, reflections, and more. If you like, try reading aloud the chapter introductions to your subject to help set the stage for what to expect next.

Together, all these pieces create a well-rounded account of a life—a life that's a critical part of your own family's story.

SOME SUGGESTIONS:

• **Make taking an oral history a family project.** The popularity of genealogy and genetic testing are sparking millions to understand the outlines of their family backgrounds. Taking an oral history is a wonderful opportunity to learn more about your family in a similar way—but this approach to ancestry colors in the rich details.

• **Appeal to a sense of heritage and giving.** The prospect of creating a written legacy for later generations to keep the flame alive may motivate your loved one to enlist in the project.

• **Compare multiple oral histories.** Recording even one parent's or grandparent's life story adds tremendously to family history and helps keep their spirit alive forever. If you're lucky enough to have other members of these generations still with you, getting each story down on paper multiplies the effect. Imagine what a treasure trove that makes for children and grandchildren. These questions are also designed to work for the oral history of a beloved aunt, uncle, godparent, mentor, or other significant figure.

• **Use the prompts as a conversation guide.** Don't expect to plow from cover to cover in a single sitting, unless you're a clan of storytellers who don't need much sleep! Revisit this journal over time. Along with creating a family keepsake, one of the greatest things about doing this is the chance to just spend thoughtful time with a loved one.

• **Start anywhere!** Some people are inclined to think chronologically, while others are inspired by big events or emotional moments like family celebrations. There's no right or wrong way to dive in. Nor do you have to fill in every single space in the book in order to have a successful oral history. This is a family endeavor, not a formal academic project. Success is managing to preserve any fragments of memory. So start at the beginning, or flip through the pages.

• **Begin sooner rather than later.** If families think about oral histories at all, it's often something to do "later." It may seem like waiting has advantages; after all, the longer a life, the more source material to mine. On the other hand, any of us, by the time we have adult children, have a life story worth committing to paper and sharing with others.

There's a risk in being too late. Time alone sloughs away many nuggets of information. Tragedy can strike unexpectedly. Memories fade. Dementia steals still more memories—and it's a condition one in three of us will develop in our lifetime. Even if your parent or grandparent is already showing signs of memory loss, it can be a terrific time to take an oral history. With Alzheimer's, new memories have trouble being formed, which is why the person forgets we just asked a question. But the farther you go back in time, the better memories of those times tend to be retained. And all of us have more vivid memories of emotionally charged experiences and relationships, from weddings and beloved pets to the music we adored in our teens. So ask away. You might be surprised with what you can still retrieve and keep safe.

In short, the ideal time to take anyone's oral history is probably yesterday. The next-best time is right now.

Tips on Taking a Personal History

FOR THE MOST PRODUCTIVE SESSIONS IN TAKING SOMEONE'S ORAL HISTORY:

• **Set a relaxing scene.** Make some tea or coffee. Turn off the TV so you can both focus. Sit in a comfy spot. Above all, give yourselves time. Pick the time of day when your subject tends to have the most energy and patience.

• **Prompt, rather than interrogate.** The whole idea is to spark memories, impressions, and conversations that you can jot down. Often one basic answer might inspire a longer story about something related or something that just pops to mind—a conversation, an event, a long-lost snippet of time. This is gold, so resist the urge to rush. Allow your subject a little thinking time. It can take a few minutes for an answer to gestate and come out.

• **Try not to correct information you know is wrong.** It's a good way to shut someone down rather than getting him or her to open up. This isn't a test. (You can always make a note to ask more about it later or put a question mark in the journal.)

• **Feel free to wander "off script."** If a particular prompt raises a story or thought you've never heard or you want to know more about a topic than a simple yes-no answer, ask questions that expand on it. Good ones to try: "Why?" "And then what happened?" "Why do you think that?" "What happened to...?" Keep some loose paper handy; if you run out of space, you can jot notes on the paper and insert it into the journal later (or use the blank pages at the back).

• **Expect the sad or the unexpected.** Not every memory or story is a happy one. That's okay. Respect your subject's level of willingness to relive these moments. You might even find yourself being touched by, or unexpectedly moved to tears by, what you hear.

• **Don't press too hard.** Follow your subject's lead. If you sense a lot of reluctance or he/she doesn't remember, just move on to another question. Maybe later you can revisit it.

• **Show your own enthusiasm.** Nod or add the occasional "mmm hmmm" just as you would in regular conversation. These subtle responses reassure a listener, even subconsciously, that you're attentive and interested.

• **Consider having some memorabilia handy as you talk.** Old photos or albums, heirlooms, yearbooks, awards, old letters, or a postcard collection can spark the mind. Or try playing the music that was popular in different bygone eras. You can even use a digital tool like Google Maps or Street View to peek at former hometowns, neighborhoods, streets, and houses.

• **Think twice about having other people in the room.** Spouses, siblings, and other listeners sometimes can't help themselves. They interject their own memories or correct what the subject is saying. They might steer the direction of stories away from what the person talking really wants to tell about. It's true that they can also provide helpful details, or might just enjoy listening. Just know going into it that having a third party around might change the tone of what you're trying to accomplish, or prep them ahead of time with ground rules.

• **Encourage reluctant subjects.** With those who are self-conscious or don't like talking about themselves, or think they have nothing important to say, emphasize the value to the broader family history. Remind them that everyone's life and perspective holds interest and meaning, from its broad outlines to the deeper insights into topics that you've never talked about before. Try turning the opportunity around: "Don't you wish you knew more about your mother's childhood (or your grandmother's life, your father's hometown, etc.)?"

*Vivid or vague,
surprising or familiar,
the information that moves from the mind
to paper tends to wind up as any family's
most treasured keepsake of all.*

CHAPTER I

Family Back Stories

ANCESTORS ON THE FAMILY TREE

*In every conceivable manner, the family is link
to our past, bridge to our future.*

ALEX HALEY

Some families know more than others about their origins and extended branches. And that's okay. Whether your knowledge goes back many generations or only one or two, sharing this information helps those who come after understand a bit more about the threads that stitch them together.

This chapter isn't meant to be a complete genealogy, just a space to hang onto the basics. You'd be surprised how much of this information slips away from us. But there may be many reasons over the years that family members wish they knew these facts.

Answer as many as you can. Other relatives or genealogy resources may be able to help fill in the rest.

*Remember, the "you" in these questions and prompts refers to
the parent, or subject, of this oral history.*

Your Family History

Where and when was your mother born?

Where and when was your father born?

Do you know the story of how your family, or you, came to this country?

Five-Generation Family Tree

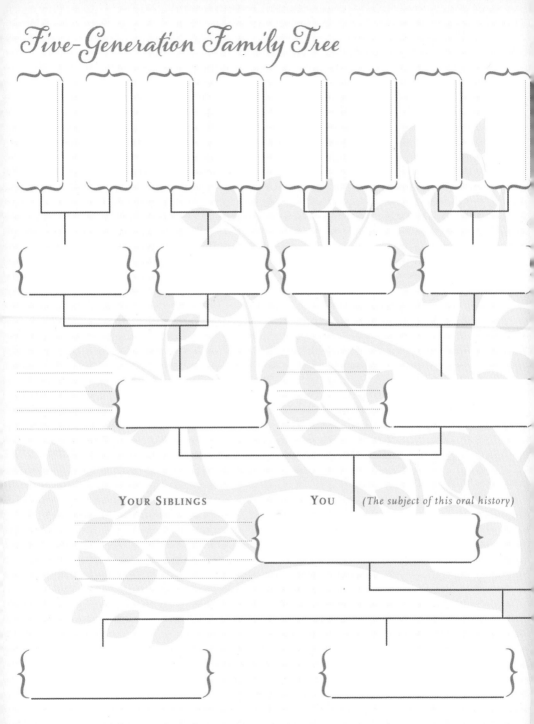

YOUR SIBLINGS

YOU *(The subject of this oral history)*

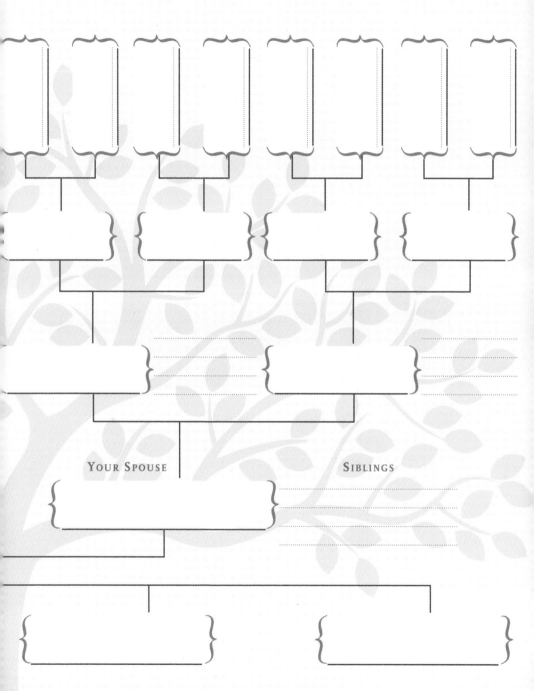

YOUR SPOUSE

SIBLINGS

How far back has anyone traced your family's roots?

Has anything surprising come up in this research?

Do you know the meaning of your family surname?

What is your ethnic ancestry?

Did you learn about your ancestry as a child or was it rarely talked about?

Have you had genetic testing done to learn about ancestry? If so, what kind of testing, and what were the notable findings?

Do you know if other relatives have done genetic ancestry testing? If so, what were the results?

Which relative on your family tree are you said to most resemble?

Which relative on your family tree are you said to be most like in personality?

Family Health History

The family health history can be important knowledge for future generations.

GENETIC OR MEDICAL CONDITIONS

You   **Condition & date/age of onset**

Your Mother's Family   **Condition & date/age of onset**

Your Father's Family   **Condition & date/age of onset**

Your Grandparents

How well did you know them when you were a child?

What were their grandparent nicknames (Grandpa, Gran, Mimi, etc.)?

Where did they live during your childhood?

Were you closer to your father's parents or your mother's?

What do you know about their childhoods?

Do you know anything about their courtships or early married life?

What did your mother's parents do for a living?

What did your father's parents do for a living?

How did you spend time with them?

What kind of influence did your grandparents have on you?

Are there special foods you associate with your grandparents?

Describe how you remember your favorite grandparent:

Are there special sayings you associate with a grandparent?

If they're deceased, do you know the cause of death?

If you could talk to them again one last time, what would you tell them?

STANDOUT MEMORIES OF YOUR GRANDPARENTS

Great-grandparents' and Grandparents' Generations

Use this page to record anything that is known about your great-grandparents and their siblings and cousins; and your grandparents' siblings and cousins. Include their names, birth dates, where they lived, and any facts or stories about them.

Your Mother

Do you know who she was named after or the story of her name?

Where did she grow up?

What were the circumstances of her childhood and upbringing that shaped her?

What did your mother do for a living?

What did your mother like to do in her free time?

Did she have any sayings she often used?

Did she have a particular look (clothing, hairstyles, etc.) that you associate with her?

What was she happiest doing?

How have your views of your mother changed over the years—how you saw her when you were a child compared to how you see her today?

What's something important you learned from your mother?

Your Father

Do you know who he was named after or the story of his name?

Where did he grow up?

What were the circumstances of his childhood and upbringing that shaped him?

In what ways do you resemble your father?

What did your father do for a living?

What did your father like to do in his free time?

Did he have any sayings he often used?

Did he have a particular look (clothing, hairstyles, etc.) that you associate with him?

What was he happiest doing?

How have your views of your father changed over the years—how you saw him when you were a child compared to how you see him today?

What's something important you learned from your father?

More About Your Parents

Whose temperament and personality is most like yours?

Which parent did you get along with best while growing up?

What kinds of things did you argue with your parents about?

Were they lenient or strict parents? How did they discipline?

What do you think were the important sensibilities they tried to instill in you?

Were your parents happy when you were growing up?

Who were your parents' best friends?

STANDOUT MEMORIES OF YOUR PARENTS

Your Siblings

How do you think your birth order affected you?

....

....

....

If you're an only child, did you wish you had siblings?

....

Did your place in the family or family size influence how many children you wanted or had?

....

....

....

Were you close to your siblings growing up?

....

....

....

Did you have a brother or sister to whom you were closest? Has that changed over time?

....

....

....

....

Do you feel your parents favored one child over another? Who?

....

....

....

....

Did you and your siblings have nicknames for one another?

Did you feel competitive?

Did you and a sibling have a secret language?

Did you ever invent special games together?

What's a secret that you and a sibling kept from your parents?

Did you wear (or pass along) hand-me-downs?

What's something you learned from a brother or sister?

Did each sibling have a different role in the family (peacemaker, troublemaker, and so on)?

Do you and your siblings still fall into childhood roles when you get together as adults?

STANDOUT SIBLING MEMORIES

Other Relatives

Was your extended family close?

Did they get together much while growing up? How?

Are there family superstitions you heard while growing up? Relatives or ancestors with unusual stories?

Were there unrelated people who were "like family"? What was their relationship to your family and how were they included?

What about cousins? Record names, birth dates, where they lived, and any facts or stories about them.

STANDOUT MEMORIES OF YOUR EXTENDED FAMILY

Family Hall of Fame

Relative who had the biggest influence on you:
....

Most interesting ancestor:
....

Ancestor with the best name:
....

Relative you most resemble:
....

Favorite aunt:
....

Favorite uncle:
....

Favorite cousin:
....

Family historian:
....

Family musician:
....

Best sense of humor:
....

Best cook:
....

Noted athlete or sportsman:
....

Family hero:
....

Biggest traveler:
....

Relative with the most unusual hobby:
....

Relative with the best pet:
....

Most famous relative:
....

Most inspiring relative:
....

Most mysterious relative:
....

CHAPTER 2

Early Days

BIRTH, CHILDHOOD, FIRST FRIENDSHIPS, EDUCATION, AND FIRST JOBS

I sometimes think that childhood is where the real meaning of life is located, and that we, adults, are its servants.

KARL OVE KNAUSGAARD

We all begin as children—and yet it can be so hard to imagine our parents and grandparents in diapers and playclothes! That's why it's important to share what we remember about our own lives. The fun of these first memories is that the harder you think about them, the more comes into focus. One image tumbles into another, often out of chronological order but with more and more delicious details.

So close your eyes and climb into the way-back machine. Conjure up as much as you can, and use the blank pages to record images that pop up but aren't covered by specific prompts.

What's your earliest memory? About how old were you and what do you recall?

Birth or Adoption

When and where were you born?

Was it in a hospital, at home, or somewhere else?

Was there anything unusual or surprising about your arrival?

Do you know who attended your birth? (your father? a midwife?)

What did you weigh and measure at birth?

Is there a story behind your name?

What have your feelings been about your name throughout life?

Is there a different name you wish you had?

If You're Adopted...

Do you know your birth parents?

If so, what (if any) is your relationship to your birth parents?

At what age (and how) did you discover you were adopted?

As a child, how did you feel about being adopted?

Have your feelings about adoption changed over time?

Childhood

Did you have a nickname growing up?

What did you call your parents (Mother and Father, Mom/Mum and Dad, etc.)?

What sort of child were you?

What three words best describe your childhood?

What was your happiest year growing up?

What's the most traumatic thing that happened to you as a child?

What chores did you do?

Describe a typical family dinner from your childhood: What might have been served? Who was at the dinner table? Were there special rituals? Who cooked and who cleaned up?

Describe a typical afternoon of play as a young child: What sorts of games did you play? What toys did you play with? Who was there? Were you supervised?

Did you play any sports?

Can you remember any of your parents' rules (curfews, no running indoors, etc.)?

How were you disciplined for breaking rules?

What's the most trouble you got into as a child?

What's the first movie you remember seeing in a movie theater?

What kinds of things did you do after school?

What's an enduring family story others tell about you?

Were you a healthy child or a sickly one?

Were you more athletic or bookish?

On a scale of 1 (solitary) to 10 (very sociable), where did you fall?

Were you in Scouting or a similar youth group? Did you enjoy it?

What did you like best about your neighborhood or hometown?

Did you have more or less freedom than your own children did?

Can you still describe your childhood bedroom?

What was your backyard or favorite play park like?

Have you ever gone back and visited the house you grew up in? What was that like?

Who took care of you besides your parents?

STANDOUT MEMORIES OF CHILDHOOD PLAY

Do you remember ... when you spent your first night away from home?

Your Favorites: Childhood List

Best friend:

Toy:

Doll or stuffed animal:

Book(s):

Movie:

TV or radio program:

Pet:

Hiding place:

Way to spend an afternoon:

Type of candy:

Breakfast cereal:

Thing to wear:

Comfort food:

Sports team:

Way to get around:

Add any details here, if you wish.

First Friendships

Who was your first best friend?

....

Who were your other childhood friends?

....

....

Are you still in touch with any childhood or school friends today?

....

....

....

Picture how you spent an afternoon with friends when you were eight years old. Describe what sorts of things you did, where you hung out, and how you got around.

....

....

....

....

Describe the same scene at age 12.

....

....

....

....

Now describe what it was like hanging out with friends at 16.

....

....

....

....

Childhood Dreams

What did you want to be when you grew up?

....

....

....

Did you expect to travel and move away or stay in your hometown?

....

....

....

Whom did you idolize?

....

....

....

How did you envision your grown-up life?

....

....

....

....

Do you remember ... **when you realized you might not achieve a childhood dream?**

....

....

....

Education

SCHOOLS ATTENDED AND DATES:

- Elementary or Primary

- Middle

- High School

- College

ABOUT ELEMENTARY OR PRIMARY SCHOOL

Which was your favorite grade, and why?

What was your favorite subject? Best subject?

Did you have a special teacher?

What kinds of clubs, sports, or activities were you involved in?

How did you spend recess?

ABOUT MIDDLE SCHOOL

Which was your favorite grade, and why?

What was your favorite subject? Best subject?

Did you ever hide a report card?

Did you have a special teacher?

What kinds of clubs, sports, or activities were you involved in?

What's something you were very proud of at school?

Do you remember ... when man first walked on the moon? Tell where you were and what that was like:

About High School

Which was your favorite grade, and why?

What was your favorite subject? Best subject?

Did you have a special teacher?

What kinds of clubs, sports, or activities were you involved in?

What's something you were very proud of at school?

What music groups were popular?

Did you go to any dances or proms? Describe the details.

AFTER HIGH SCHOOL

What did you do right after high school?

What trade, vocational training, travel, marriage, or other options were available to you? If you chose an option other than college or military service, recount the details.

Do you remember ... when there were no personal computers? What was that like? How did you write school reports before the Internet?

About College

How did you decide where to go?

What did you major in or study there?

How did you pay for college?

What was college like for you?

Did you meet anyone in college you still know today?

What kinds of clubs, sports, or activities were you involved in?

Did you go to graduate school?

Do you remember ... having your first drink?

STANDOUT MEMORIES FROM COLLEGE

Military Service

Date of enlistment: ....

Date of discharge: ....

Branch of service: ....

Rank and unit: ....

Why did you enlist?

How did you choose your branch of service?

How did your family and friends react?

Where you did basic training:

What was the hardest part of basic training?

Where were you stationed and what were these places like? What do you remember best about them?

Which experience in the military was most meaningful to you?

What were some of your responsibilities?

Conflicts served in:

Decorations or awards:

Have you stayed in touch with those you served with?

What did you learn from your military service?

STANDOUT MEMORIES OF MILITARY SERVICE

First Jobs

What was your first job and what did you do?

....

....

....

How old were you, and how did you get the job?

....

....

....

What did you spend your first paycheck on?

....

....

....

What were your other earliest jobs?

....

....

....

....

....

....

....

....

CHAPTER 3

Milestone Moments

LIFE'S MAJOR EVENTS

The events in our lives happen in a sequence in time,
but in their significance to ourselves they find their own order.

EUDORA WELTY

Although life is lived in the "little moments," it's the big events that shape its broad outlines. That's why history pays so much attention to life-changing milestones.

These prompts not only record the basics, they tend to provide a good jumping-off place for organizing memories because it's often easier to recall the big stuff. These prompts will also get you thinking chronologically about major happenings in your life.

Were there any scholarships, travel opportunities, accidents, illnesses, deaths, or other circumstances that you think altered the course of your life? Describe them here:

....

....

....

....

Love

Who was your first crush and how old were you?

Who was your first boyfriend/girlfriend?

Did you go on lots of dates or were you a late bloomer?

Who was the most significant (pre-marriage) romantic partner?

How did you meet your spouse?

What was your courtship like? Was it love at first sight or something slower to develop?

How did you decide to marry?

How did your parents and friends react?

How long was the engagement?

STANDOUT ROMANTIC MEMORIES

WORDS OF ADVICE ... On how, where, and when to find Mr. or Ms. "Right":

Marriage

THE WEDDING

Date: Time:

Ceremony location:

Reception location:

Officiate:

Best man:

Maid-of-honor:

Other attendants:

Who planned and paid for the wedding?

How many attended?

Describe the wedding ceremony, including special music or vows, flowers and décor:

What did you wear?

....

....

Traditions you kept (or not):

....

....

....

Describe the reception, including music, flowers and décor, menu and cake:

....

....

....

....

....

....

....

....

Were there any noteworthy toasts or speeches?

....

....

....

....

What was your favorite part of the day?

Did anything unexpected happen?

Were there other events connected to the wedding?

What would you have done differently?

WORDS OF ADVICE ... On what makes a good wedding:

....

....

....

....

....

....

WORDS OF ADVICE ... On what makes a great marriage:

....

....

....

....

....

....

....

Do you remember ... the weddings in which you were an attendant? Whose were they and what was your role?

....

....

....

....

....

....

Honeymoon

If you took one, where did you go?

What is your favorite honeymoon memory?

Who planned (and paid for) the honeymoon?

If you didn't take one, why not? What did you do instead?

WORDS OF ADVICE ... For a newlywed couple:

STANDOUT WEDDING AND HONEYMOON MEMORIES

(This space can also be used for describing a second wedding and honeymoon, if relevant.)

Children

Include such details as: name, birth date and time, location, city/state, who attended the birth, who picked the name (and why), what the birth was like, and first impressions.

Child #1:

Child #2:

Child #3:

Others:

Did you always expect you'd have children?

Did you ever want more children than you had?

Do you remember ... each child's first word? First steps?

For mothers: Did you like being pregnant?

For fathers: What do you remember most about pregnancy?

What was it like to see each of your children for the first time?

Which ages in your children's lives have you enjoyed the most?

Describe each child in three words:

Do you remember ... when you felt proudest of each child?

WORDS OF ADVICE ... **On parenting:**

Grandchildren

Name/birth date:

Name/birth date:

Name/birth date:

Name/birth date:

Name/birth date:

Name/birth date:

Name/birth date:

When did you first meet your first grandchild?

What do your grandchildren call you?

Is grandparenthood all it's cracked up to be?

Do you like to babysit a grandchild?

Do you remember ... how you found out you were going to be a grandparent?

STANDOUT GRANDPARENTING MEMORIES

Other Life-Changing Moments

Were you ever written about in the newspaper? Appear on TV? (Tell why, when.)

What's the first concert you ever attended?

What's the first live theatre performance you ever saw?

Did you ever have the experience of hearing a life-changing lecture, speech, or sermon?

Do you remember ... watching the Olympics for the first time?

Yes or No? Did you ever...

Experience a natural disaster?

Visit the emergency room as a patient?

Have your passport stolen?

Make a hole in one golfing?

Win big at the casino?

Total your car?

Have your wallet stolen?

Cry at a movie?

Serve on a jury?

Gone to a professional sports event?

Add details of any "yes" answers here, if you wish.

Religious Milestones

Use this page to record events such as baptisms, confirmations, bat/bar mitzvahs, or other ceremonies and events.

Do-Overs!

HERE'S YOUR CHANCE TO INDULGE IN A LITTLE "WHAT-IF" THINKING.

School(s) I wish I'd attended:

Subject I wish I'd studied:

Job or career I might have preferred:

Trip I wish I'd taken:

Place I wish I'd lived:

Place I wish I lived right now:

Other regrets:

Do you remember ... when 9/11 happened? Where were you?

CHAPTER 4

Everyday Life

PRESERVING A PEEK AT THE ROUTINES THAT MARK THE DAYS

Even very ordinary people, upon closer examination,
can often look extraordinary.

HOLLY HUNTER

When we read a novel or watch a movie, the plot is the driver of the story. All those high points and action keep us following along. But it's the settings and the ways the characters connect with one another that we often can't get enough of—and that stay with us for a long time after. They make the whole thing alive.

These prompts encourage a closer look at "daily life," the backgrounds, routines, and relationships of family life.

On Everyday Routines

What's your morning routine?

....

....

What's your bedtime routine?

....

....

What other routines or habits mark your days?

....

On Your Homes

LIST YOUR MOST MEMORABLE HOMES

LOCATION: .... **Years:** ....

Description of home: ....

....

....

....

LOCATION: .... **Years:** ....

Description of home: ....

....

....

....

LOCATION: .... **Years:** ....

Description of home: ....

....

....

....

LOCATION: .... **Years:** ....

Description of home: ....

....

....

LOCATION: .... **Years:** ....

Description of home: ....

....

What do you remember best about the home you were born into?

What was the first place you lived as an independent adult and what was that like?

How did you pick the first home you bought? What drew you to it? Can you describe the floor plan, the style, the view, the backyard, how many floors?

Which home was your favorite ever, and why?

What's your favorite spot in your present home, and what do you love about it?

If you've ever lived in another country, what did you appreciate about living there?

If you could live anywhere in the world, where would it be, and why?

Standout Memories of Your Homes

Do you remember ... what life was like with only a few TV channels?

Yes or no? Do you enjoy this aspect of home life?

Cooking?

Decorating?

Cleaning?

Organizing?

Painting walls?

Mowing the lawn?

Paying bills?

Hanging pictures?

Gardening?

Add details of any "yes" answers here, if you wish.

Words of Advice ... On choosing a place to live:

On Your Work

WORK HISTORY

JOB TITLE: Dates:

Employer: Location:

Memories and Experiences:

JOB TITLE: Dates:

Employer: Location:

Memories and Experiences:

JOB TITLE: Dates:

Employer: Location:

Memories and Experiences:

JOB TITLE: Dates:

Employer: Location:

Memories and Experiences:

JOB TITLE: Dates:

Employer: Location:

Memories and Experiences:

WORDS OF ADVICE ... **On managing a career:**

WORDS OF ADVICE ... **On the definition of success:**

On Being a Spouse

In what ways do you and your partner complement one another?

What have been the highlights of your marriage?

What sorts of compromises did you have to make in your relationship?

What has been challenging, and how did you handle that?

WORDS OF ADVICE ... On what makes a good relationship:

On Being a Parent

Was becoming a parent what you imagined, or different? How so?

What was harder than you anticipated?

What was easier?

Describe your parenting style:

Did you and your partner have similar approaches to and philosophies about parenting, or were they different? How did this work out?

Tell about a specific time a child made you feel you'd done well as a parent.

Tell about a specific time a child surprised you.

What was the most challenging part of raising a child?

What was the most pleasurable part of raising a child?

WORDS OF ADVICE ... On raising kids:

Describe some family traditions you've cherished:

Bedtime routines

Saturday mornings

A special meal

Summer evenings

The first day of school

The last day of school

What else?

Words of Advice ... Your most important job as a parent is:

Did you consciously parent in ways similar to how you were brought up, or were you deliberately different? How so?

Did your children become the people you imagined they would?

STANDOUT MEMORIES OF THE CHILD-REARING YEARS

On Being Part of a Community

MEMBERSHIPS...

...In civic groups (what, when, your role):

...As a volunteer (what, when, your role):

...In religious organizations (what, when, your role):

...In other community groups (book clubs, coaching, social circles, etc.):

What does "community" mean to you?

In what ways do you feel you have been a good citizen?

CHAPTER 5

Celebrations

BIRTHDAYS, HOLIDAYS, REUNIONS, AND TRAVEL

*The more you praise and celebrate your life,
the more there is in life to celebrate.*

OPRAH WINFREY

*P*ut on a party hat! Smell the good things cooking! Remember how it felt the first time you boarded a plane or whenever you hit the open road! The celebratory times in life linger long in our memories because they're associated with so many positives: flavors, scents, special clothes or decorations, togetherness, excitement, happiness.

Most every family celebrates a handful of special days in the year. They may vary in their importance within each household, but we all celebrate them, and we all pass along traditions.

Birthdays

Describe your ideal birthday:

....

....

....

....

What are the family birthday traditions you usually follow?

....

....

....

....

Are they different for children?

....

....

....

What's your favorite birthday cake?

....

....

Have you ever been thrown a surprise party? If so, did you like it? Describe what happened.

....

....

....

....

....

Did you have a 16th birthday party or quinceañera?

How did you celebrate your 21st birthday?

How did you celebrate your 50th birthday?

Which birthday was your most fun?

What's the best present you ever received?

What's the best present you ever gave?

Would you rather be the birthday celebrant or the planner?

STANDOUT BIRTHDAY MEMORIES

Holidays

Which holiday do you most look forward to and why?

....

....

....

EASTER OR PASSOVER

How you spend the day:

....

....

Special foods?

....

....

Special decorations?

....

....

Special clothing?

....

....

It wouldn't be the holiday without this:

....

....

Tradition carried on from your parents:

....

....

Most memorable year of this holiday:

....

....

Which holiday do you dread and why?

HALLOWEEN

Your best costume ever as a child:

Your best costume ever as an adult:

Special foods:

Special decorations:

It wouldn't be the holiday without this:

Most memorable year of this holiday:

Thanksgiving

How you spend the day:

Special foods:

Special decorations:

It wouldn't be the holiday without this:

Tradition carried on from your parents:

Most memorable year of this holiday:

CHRISTMAS, HANUKKAH, AND OTHER WINTER HOLIDAYS

How you spend the day(s):

Special foods?

Special decorations?

Special clothing?

It wouldn't be the holiday without this:

Tradition carried on from your parents:

Most memorable year of this holiday:

New Year's Eve

How you celebrate:

Special foods?

Special decorations?

Special clothing?

It wouldn't be the holiday without this:

Most memorable year of this holiday:

If you celebrate St. Patrick's Day, Mother's Day, Father's Day, Independence Day, Eid al-Fitr, Rosh Hashanah, Yom Kippur, Kwanzaa, Chinese New Year, or other holidays that are special to you, record details here:

Favorites: The Holiday List

Valentine's gift:

Easter or Passover dish:

Halloween tradition:

Thanksgiving dish:

Holiday cookie:

Holiday song:

Holiday treat:

Holiday movie:

Place to be on New Year's Eve:

Celebratory cocktail:

Add any details here, if you wish.

Holiday Recipes Worth Preserving

Jot down one or two family classics here so they're never forgotten.

Reunions

Describe a memorable family reunion:

Did you ever attend a school reunion? Tell about it:

Did you ever attend a work-related reunion? Tell about it:

Travel

Do you consider yourself a traveler or a homebody?

Are you a planner or a wanderer?

Light packer or pack rat?

Window or aisle seat?

Do you prefer to revisit old favorites or find new destinations?

Best vacation of all time:

Most romantic vacation you've had:

One of the better family vacations you took:

Have you ever traveled alone? Where, and what was it like?

Farthest you've ever traveled?

Favorite places you've visited:

Other places still on your wish list:

Have you ever kept a travel diary?

Souvenir you're glad you bought:

How has travel changed your sense of yourself?

How has travel changed your sense of the world?

Name all the countries you've traveled to. Add details.

Favorites: The Travel List

Mode of transport:

Country:

City:

Particular place:

Beach:

National park:

Hotel:

Travel companion:

Add any details here, if you wish.

Do you remember ... when you first saw the ocean?

_____

_____

_____

_____

Do you remember ... when you first saw snow?

_____

_____

_____

_____

WORDS OF ADVICE ... On what makes a good trip:

_____

_____

_____

_____

_____

_____

_____

CHAPTER 6

More About You

YOUR INTERESTS, BELIEFS, FRIENDSHIPS, AND MORE

To be yourself in a world that is constantly trying to make you something else is the greatest accomplishment.

RALPH WALDO EMERSON

No one sees us the way we see ourselves. Friends, family, co-workers, and strangers often see the outermost version that we present to the world. Even when they know us pretty well, they might not know how we'd answer certain questions or what our exact take on the world is.

This chapter explores and celebrates what helps make you uniquely... YOU.

All You

Do you consider yourself an introvert or an extrovert?

Do you consider yourself more optimistic or pessimistic?

Name three adjectives that people who know you best would use to describe you:

Name three adjectives that you would use to describe yourself:

What trait would you change about yourself if you could?

If you've ever done any personality testing (Myers-Briggs, etc.), what did it find?

If you could choose a superpower, what would it be?

What do you like best about your appearance?

What has the physical side of getting older been like for you?

What are your thoughts and practices about wellness (diet, exercise, sleep, etc.)?

Is there a book you've read over and over? What do you get from it?

A movie you've watched repeatedly? Why?

What has your relationship to money been throughout your life? Has it changed over time?

What's your greatest extravagance?

What words or phrases do you frequently use?

Interests & Skills

What attracted you to your favorite hobby, sport, or pastime?

Are there recreational activities you still do, and any you've abandoned?

Have you ever created something that you're especially proud of?

Do you have a hidden talent?

WORDS OF ADVICE ... **On how to be "healthy, wealthy, and wise":**

Yes or no? Do you know how to...

Play a musical instrument?

Speak a foreign language?

Bake bread?

Change the oil in the car?

Paint?

Wiggle your ears?

Waltz?

Knit?

Drive a stick shift?

Use a slide rule?

Make a fire?

Play poker?

Use social media?

Add details of any "yes" answers here, if you wish.

Spiritual Beliefs

What is your faith or denomination?

How do you practice your religion in your daily life?

How important has your spiritual life been to the rest of your life?

Have your feelings about religion evolved over time?

WORDS OF ADVICE ... What's the best advice anyone ever gave you?

Political Beliefs

Are you a registered member of a political party? Which party do you most identify with?

....

....

Which candidates for major office did you vote for over the years?

....

....

....

Do you vote in every election? Ever regret a vote?

....

....

Have you ever volunteered for a campaign?

....

....

Have you ever run for office yourself?

....

....

....

What causes are you most passionate about supporting?

....

....

....

Do you remember ... what it was like the first time you voted? Who did you vote for?

....

....

....

Other Beliefs

Do you believe in luck? Why or why not?

Do you believe in fate? Coincidence? Why or why not?

Do you believe in astrology?

What's your general philosophy on life?

What's your motto?

WORDS OF ADVICE ... If you're going to break a rule, make it this one:

YES OR NO? HAVE YOU EVER...

Dyed your hair?

Parachuted from a plane?

Been arrested?

Smoked cigarettes?

Rock climbed?

Been in a car accident?

Broken someone's heart?

Ridden a motorcycle?

Had plastic surgery?

Had an addiction to something?

Spoken to a large audience?

Add details of any "yes" answers here, if you wish.

Friends and Acquaintances

Who are your current closest friends?

Who has been your friend the longest?

How do you like to spend time with friends?

Have you found it hard or easy to make friends? Has this changed as you've gotten older?

What qualities do you most value in a friend?

WORDS OF ADVICE ... On the best way to be a good friend:

Favorites: The People List

Friend:

Neighbor:

Actor:

Actress:

Character in a book or movie:

Author:

Artist:

Columnist:

Singer:

Musical group:

President:

Historical figure:

Pro athlete:

Sportscaster:

Personal hero:

Add any details here, if you wish.

CHAPTER 7

The Stuff of Life

LET'S NOT FORGET CARS, RECIPES, FASHION, HEIRLOOMS ...

*Nothing can be so perfect while we possess it
as it will seem when remembered.*

OLIVER WENDELL HOLMES, JR.

Whether you consider yourself an enthusiastic collector and treasurer of material goods or not very materialistic at all, things do mark our lives. They're our companions along life's way. They remind us of people and places. They can be magical talismans that represent luck and hope or commemorative objects that conjure up memory and love.

This chapter is all about the concrete things that have accompanied you along life's way: purchases made, foods eaten, clothing worn, and objects treasured.

Cars

When did you learn to drive?

....

....

What was the first car you owned (year, make, model, color)?

....

....

What other memorable vehicles have you owned?

....

....

Have you given any of your cars nicknames?

....

....

What dream car would you be driving right now if money were no object?

....

....

What's the wildest driving adventure you've had?

....

....

....

....

WORDS OF ADVICE ... On buying a car:

....

....

....

....

Food

First dish you ever learned how to cook:

....

....

Food from your past that you'd love to dig into now:

....

....

....

Your mother's most delicious dish:

....

....

Your grandmother's signature dish:

....

....

Mealtime memories:

....

....

....

When would your family go out to eat, and what was that like?

....

....

....

Do you remember ... when you ate your first elegant restaurant meal?

....

....

....

Special Family Recipes

What would your mother serve you when you were sick?

What are your favorite dishes for:

• Breakfast?

• Lunch?

• Dinner?

Have you ever followed a special or unusual diet?

What are some of the foods that are always in your pantry? Were any also particular to your mother's pantry?

Most memorable restaurant meal:

Do you prefer to entertain or be a guest?

Your go-to dinner party menu:

Favorites: Foods

Type of cereal:

Vegetable and fruit:

Dessert:

Late-night snack:

Soup:

Way to cook eggs:

Flavor of ice cream:

Cookie and cake:

Candy:

Type of ethnic cuisine:

Non-alcoholic beverage:

Alcoholic beverage:

Add any details here, if you wish.

Fashion

Do you wear anything that belonged to your parents?

What did you mostly wear as a teenager?

What did you mostly wear as a young parent?

Fill in the blank: You can never have too many _____.

Is there a memorable item of clothing you've worn?

Do you have a piece of jewelry with a special story behind it?

What's the oldest piece of jewelry or clothing you own? Why have you had it so long?

WORDS OF ADVICE ... On projecting an appearance:

Heirlooms and Special Things

Do you consider yourself sentimental about objects? Elaborate.

COLLECTING

What do you collect?

How did the collecting begin?

What's your best "find" of all time?

What are the characteristics of an object that make you want to add it to your collection?

Are there pieces of your collection that have special significance?

Heritage

Did you inherit special objects from relatives?

What's your most prized possession that was your mother's?

What's your most prized possession that was your father's?

Which toys or other objects from your childhood do you still own?

Are there particular things you would like to pass on to certain individuals?

OTHER KEEPSAKES

Tell about a piece of artwork you own that's particularly important to you:

If you have a cedar chest, what's in it and why have you saved those special things?

Why do you display the particular family pictures that you do?

What, if any, old letters have you saved? Whose are they and why did you hang onto them?

What five things would you grab first in a fire?

Favorites: A List of Things

Model of car:

Flower and tree:

Animal:

Gemstone:

Movie:

Book:

Section of the newspaper:

Perfume or cologne:

Type of footwear:

Store:

Object in your home:

Invention:

Add any details here, if you wish.

CHAPTER 8

Thoughts & Reflections

WHAT DO YOU THINK ABOUT...?

I am not one of those who in expressing opinions confine themselves to facts.

MARK TWAIN

You might find this the most fun part of this journal—or the hardest. Your perspective on these prompts is likely to rest in how much you like to share your opinions and feelings. However you feel about this kind of sharing, rest assured that everyone else will welcome your taking the time to do so.

Mostly consisting of open-ended prompts, with a little extra space to record the answers, this chapter covers your beliefs, impressions, regrets, joys, wishes, advice, and the meaning of your life. Whether your answers are readily accessible or not, these ideas are brewing around inside each of us. Reach in and see what comes to mind.

At what time of life, and where, were you happiest?

At what time of life were you the most stressed?

Tell about one day of your life that you'd love to experience again:

Tell about one day of your life that you'd change, if only you could:

Which decade have you liked best (so far)?

What do you think is the biggest difference between your children's generation and yours?

How have things changed for the better in this country since you were growing up?

How have things changed for the worse since you were growing up?

What about your life has made you the most satisfied?

What do you worry about?

Three things that matter most in life are:

Three things that matter least are:

What is something that you feel you learned too late in life?

What's your attitude about getting older?

Where do you see yourself in five years?

Which person, living or dead, would you most like to have dinner with?

What are your three biggest regrets?

WORDS OF ADVICE ... Something I learned the hard way:

Congratulations! You've just won $1 million! How do you spend it?

Where would you like to go, and with whom, if money and time were no object?

What in your life are you proudest of?

What are you most grateful for?

What or who would you like to come back as, if you could?

How have you carried the family flame?

How do you want to be remembered?

What do you consider your legacy?

WORDS OF ADVICE ... A letter to my grandchild (or a future child):

Favorites: A Random List

Color:

Smell:

Season of the year:

Time of day:

Pet:

Bird:

Music:

Thing to listen to while driving:

Guilty pleasure:

Way to unwind:

Joke:

Quotation or saying:

Add any details here, if you wish.

Parting Thoughts and Memories

> *No memory*
> *is ever alone; it's at the end of*
> *a trail of memories, a dozen trails that each*
> *have their own associations.*

—Louis L'Amour

About the Author

Paula Spencer Scott is the author of *Surviving Alzheimer's: Practical Tips and Soul-Saving Wisdom for Caregivers* and other books, including, with her daughter Page, the guided journal *Like Mother, Like Daughter: A Discovery Journal for the Two of Us*. She writes often about family and health—and has kept a journal since age nine.